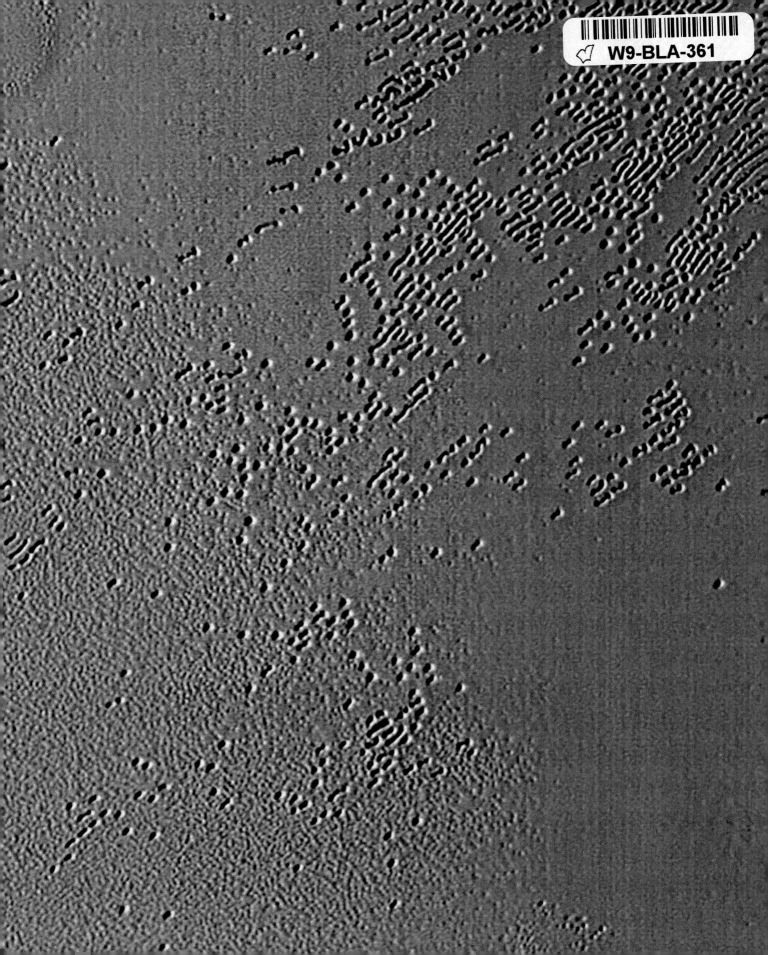

ENDPAPERS: A close-up of the icy surface of Sputnik Planitia.

TO PLUTO & BEYOND

THE AMAZING VOYAGE OF NEW HORIZONS

Elaine Scott

VIKING

For my daughter, Susan,
who always looks toward new horizons, with love . . .

Thanks to my wonderful team at Viking, Janet Pascal, Jim Hoover, and Ken Wright,
for their enthusiastic support of this project and the research that went into it. Thank you, too, to Dr. Alan Stern,
for interesting conversation and completely astounding revelations about Pluto and its companions in space.

VIKING
An imprint of Penguin Random House LLC
375 Hudson Street
New York, New York 10014

First published in the United States of America by Viking,
an imprint of Penguin Random House LLC, 2018
Copyright © 2018 by Elaine Scott

LIBRARY OF CONGRESS CATALOGING-IN-PUBLICATION DATA
Names: Scott, Elaine, date- author.
Title: To Pluto and beyond : the amazing voyage of New Horizons / by Elaine Scott.
Description: New York : Viking, Published by Penguin Group, [2018] |
Audience: Ages 8–12. | Audience: Grades 4 to 6. |
Identifiers: LCCN 2017040600 (print) | LCCN 2017042745 (ebook) | ISBN
9780451479433 (ebook) | ISBN 9781101997017 (hardcover)
Subjects: LCSH: New Horizons (Spacecraft)—Juvenile literature. | Space
probes—Juvenile literature. | Trans-Neptunian objects—Juvenile
literature. | Pluto (Dwarf planet)—Juvenile literature. | Outer
space—Exploration—Juvenile literature.
Classification: LCC QB701 (ebook) | LCC QB701 .S356 2018 (print) | DDC
629.43/54922—dc23

Book design by Jim Hoover   Set in Adobe Caslon Pro   Manufactured in China

1   3   5   7   9   10   8   6   4   2

PHOTO CREDITS
pp. ii–iii, iv–v, 23, 25, 31, 32–33, 34, 35, 36, 37, 38, 39, 40, 41, 47, 53, NASA/Johns Hopkins University Applied Physics Laboratory/Southwest
Research Institute; pp. viii, 2, 8, 9, 16, 20, 22, NASA; p. 3, Dr. R. Albrecht, European Space Agency/ESO Space Telescope European Coordinating
Facility/NASA; p. 5, NASA/Aubrey Gemignani; p. 6, SwRI/JHUAPL; pp. 10, 12, 13, Lowell Observatory Archives; p. 14, NASA/Jet Propulsion
Laboratory-Caltech; p. 15, NASA/Charles Bolden; p. 17, Lunar and Planetary Institute at the University of Arizona; p. 18, MIT/Erlend Aas/Kavli
Prize; p. 19, European Southern Observatory; p. 21, NASA/Space Telescope Science Institute; pp. 26–27, NASA/JPL/Caltech/SwRI/MSSS/Roman
Thachenko; pp. 28, 29, NASA/JPL/University of Arizona; p. 30, NASA, ESA, and the Hubble Heritage Team, Space Telescope Science Institute/
Association of Universities for Research in Astronomy; p. 42, NASA/ESA/G. Bacon Space Telescope Science Institute; p. 43, JHUAPL; p. 44,
NASA/JHUAPL/SwRI/Henry Throop; p. 45, NASA/SpacePlace; p. 46, J. Bally (University of Colorado) and H. Throop (SwRI); p. 49, NASA/ESA

CONTENTS

INTRODUCTION

ON JANUARY 19, 2006, at precisely 2:00 p.m., a spacecraft—the fastest ever launched from Earth—roared off Complex 41 at the Cape Canaveral Air Force Station in Florida. In forty-two minutes it was traveling at an astonishing 36,373 miles (600 kilometers) per hour, streaking past Earth's moon in less than nine hours! (By comparison, in 1969, it took Neil Armstrong and the crew of *Apollo 11* three *days* to get there.) Its name was New Horizons, and the moon was not its destination. It was headed much farther—all the way to Pluto, which is 3,060,000,000—3.06 billion—miles (4.9 billion kilometers) away. The unmanned spacecraft was in a hurry. Pluto was waiting to be explored, and timing was important.

Actually, Pluto was not waiting. It was on the move. Like all celestial bodies in our solar system, Pluto travels in an orbit—or path—around the sun. However, unlike the planets in Earth's solar system, which orbit the sun in an almost circular path, Pluto's pattern is a tilted oval. Usually Pluto is farther away from the sun than any of the planets. But because of the shape of its orbit, sometimes it moves nearer to the sun—even closer than Neptune, the

The Atlas 5 rocket that launched New Horizons, with its boosters, weighed 2,451,810 pounds at launch and was 196 feet tall.

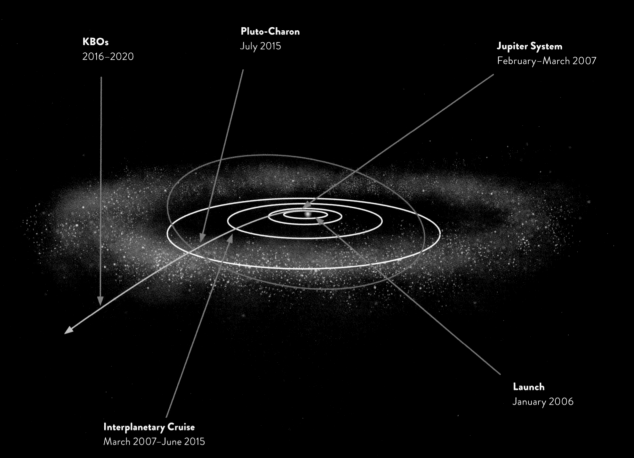

KBOs
2016–2020

Pluto-Charon
July 2015

Jupiter System
February–March 2007

Launch
January 2006

Interplanetary Cruise
March 2007–June 2015

next closest planet. Pluto moves at an average speed of 10,600 miles (17,000 kilometers) per hour, so it takes about 248 years to make one orbit of the sun. Earth races compared to Pluto, traveling 67,000 miles (107,900 kilometers) per hour and taking only a single year to complete its orbit.

At the time New Horizons launched, Pluto was speeding away from the sun's warmth.

Things were getting colder on the icy space rock. Soon its thin atmosphere, which scientists were eager to study, would freeze and fall to the ground as "snow." Not only would this snow cover up interesting surface features, it would also make the atmosphere itself more difficult to study as Pluto entered into its cold phase, which lasts for many years, and not months as winter does on Earth.

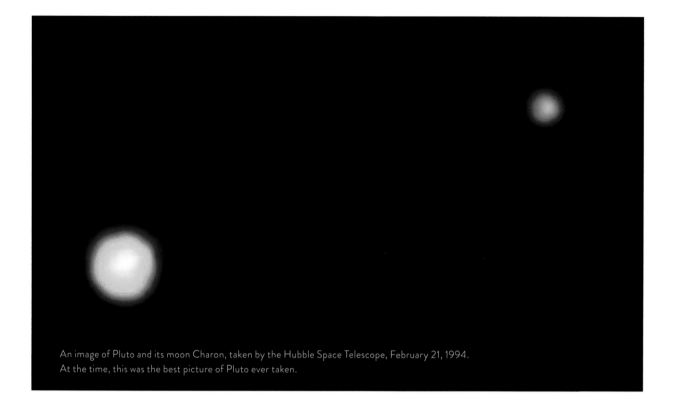

An image of Pluto and its moon Charon, taken by the Hubble Space Telescope, February 21, 1994. At the time, this was the best picture of Pluto ever taken.

Not only was it getting colder, it was also getting darker, as Pluto moved away from the sun's light. There were wonderful cameras on board New Horizons, but cameras need light in order to take clear pictures. Astronomers on Earth were eager to see good pictures of Pluto and its largest moon, Charon, in order to map their surfaces.

Timing was important, too. Planetary scientists can calculate exactly where all the planets are at any time as they travel around the sun. New Horizons needed to launch at a time when it could pass close to Jupiter as it made its way toward Pluto. By flying close to the gas giant, New Horizons would get a speed boost from Jupiter's gravity. If New Horizons missed this opportunity for the "gravity assist," as NASA (National Aeronautics and Space Administration) calls it, it would take the spacecraft an extra three to five years to reach Pluto.

The time was right, and the spacecraft was ready. No one wanted to wait. The best time to launch was January 2006. After years of careful planning, New Horizons was ready to boldly go where no spacecraft from Earth had ever been before.

1
ABOUT NEW HORIZONS

NEW HORIZONS SEEMS an appropriate name for this mission to Pluto, since "horizon" usually means the limit to how far we can see. For example, on Earth, the horizon is the line where land or sea meets the sky. Because of the curvature of the Earth, human eyes cannot see beyond that point. Due to this natural limit to their vision, some early human societies concluded that the Earth was flat and stopped at the horizon.

Fortunately, it is the nature of humans to be curious about their world. This curiosity led the ancient Greeks to discover that the Earth was round. Then, in the seventeenth century, English physicist and mathematician Sir Isaac Newton realized that some force must be acting to make objects fall to the earth and keep them there, and to keep the moon from flying away

from the Earth. He called that force *gravity*.

With each new discovery, the "horizon" of scientific knowledge expanded. And New Horizons was designed to push the boundaries of our knowledge about Pluto and the other objects in our solar system beyond anything anyone had ever known.

Dr. Alan Stern is the mission's principal investigator. He remembers becoming interested in space science when he was around seven or eight years old. Born in 1957, he was eleven when he watched humans land on the moon in the Apollo program. That mission was when he knew he wanted to be part of space exploration. Now he is.

"We're in the space exploration business," he said—though, thinking of all that we still

haven't seen, he added, "We haven't explored it very well." He was talking about the Kuiper (KY-per) Belt, a region of our solar system that is billions of miles away, beyond the planets, and is home to Pluto and millions of other icy and rocky objects. Astronomers, including Dr. Stern, think those objects in the Kuiper Belt could be leftovers from the formation of our solar system and the planets we are familiar with—including Earth. They are, in a way, fossils that will help us understand the formation of our solar system, similar to the way the fossils of dinosaurs tell us the story of their time on Earth.

It wasn't easy to get New Horizons approved,

much less off the ground. Scientists who wanted to explore Pluto had to overcome opponents who said it couldn't be done, others who said it was too expensive, and still more who said the spacecraft could never be ready in time for the crucial January 2006 launch time frame. It took years to persuade NASA that this was not an impossible mission. Fortunately, Alan Stern didn't give up, and in 2001, he and his team from the Southwest Research Institute in Boulder, Colorado, finally gained NASA's go-ahead. A mission to Pluto was possible. Dr. Stern was delighted. He said, "We are the first mission to the last planet." The "we" he was

Alan Stern, who has been interested in space since he was a child, poses with a favorite bumper sticker.

Women make up about 25 percent of the New Horizons Mission Team. This image was taken at the Applied Physics Laboratory at Johns Hopkins University, three days before New Horizons arrived at Pluto.

talking about were the 2,500 men and women who worked together to expand the horizon of scientific knowledge by designing and building a spacecraft that would turn Pluto from a mysterious dot on a fuzzy photograph into a real world billions of miles away.

Now the New Horizons team—which included NASA and other scientists and engineers from the Johns Hopkins Applied Physics Laboratory, Lockheed Martin, and International Launch Services among others—had only four years and two months to design, build, and test the spacecraft and its instruments! Everyone on the team worked together over nights and weekends in order to meet the crucial deadline. It took a lot of persistence, but they succeeded.

Everyone knew the unmanned spacecraft

had to be small and light—and it is. At 83 inches long and 108 inches wide (211 centimeters long and 274 centimeters wide), New Horizons is about the size of a baby grand piano. At launch, it weighed in at 1,054 pounds (478 kilograms). For a spacecraft, New Horizons was a real lightweight. However, it was attached to an Atlas rocket that included five rocket boosters, greatly increasing the weight. When New Horizons left the launch pad, 1.26 million pounds (571,526 kilograms) were lifted into space. Most of that weight was fuel, and the rest was the weight of the seven scientific instruments that had been created and were now on board.

They all have interesting names. Most are acronyms, names created from the first letters of the long scientific names given to the instruments. However, two instruments work together and were named after characters in a 1950s television show, *The Honeymooners*—Alice and Ralph Kramden.

Alice is a spectrometer, designed to investigate the composition and structure of the atmosphere that surrounds Pluto. It was also used to study Pluto's largest moon, Charon, to determine if it, too, had an atmosphere. A spectrometer separates light into its various wavelengths, the way raindrops split white light into rays of colored light, producing a rainbow. Alice worked in the ultraviolet wavelengths of Pluto's atmosphere. As the instrument was pointed toward a target, a series of complicated processes produced a different type of spectrum. Each spectrum revealed one of the different atoms and molecules in Pluto's atmosphere.

Alice's companion instrument, Ralph, was designed to take pictures and make the first accurate maps of Pluto and its moons. Another spectrometer inside Ralph looked for gases, frozen water, and material containing carbon, hydrogen, or oxygen atoms anywhere sunlight hit the surface of Pluto or its moons.

REX (Radio Science Experiment) is a small printed circuit board that can measure the temperature and the pressure in the atmospheres of Pluto and Charon. It can also be used to detect

the masses, or weights, of Pluto, Charon, and possibly other Kuiper Belt Objects (KBOs).

LORRI (Long Range Reconnaissance Imager) has the best vision on board New Horizons. Basically, it is a very powerful digital camera fitted with an equally powerful telescope. It can operate in the frigid temperatures surrounding Pluto which may be as low as -193 degrees Fahrenheit (-125 degrees Celsius). Astronomers—and practically everyone else—were eager to see the images LORRI would take of this strange world.

SWAP stands for Solar Wind at Pluto. This instrument measures the way Pluto reacts to the solar wind—the charged particles that come streaming from the sun. SWAP also measures how fast Pluto's atmosphere is escaping into outer space. No one knew Pluto *had* an atmosphere until 1988, when astronomers discovered evidence of it as they observed Pluto passing in front of a distant star. As Pluto passed the star, astronomers noted that the shadow cast by the tiny planet didn't have a sharp edge. Instead, Pluto's edges appeared blurred or fuzzy. Astronomers assumed the fuzz was caused by gases in an atmosphere that surrounded Pluto. However, at that time, they had no idea how much atmosphere Pluto had. They thought it didn't have much at all.

PEPSSI, or Pluto Energetic Particle Spec-

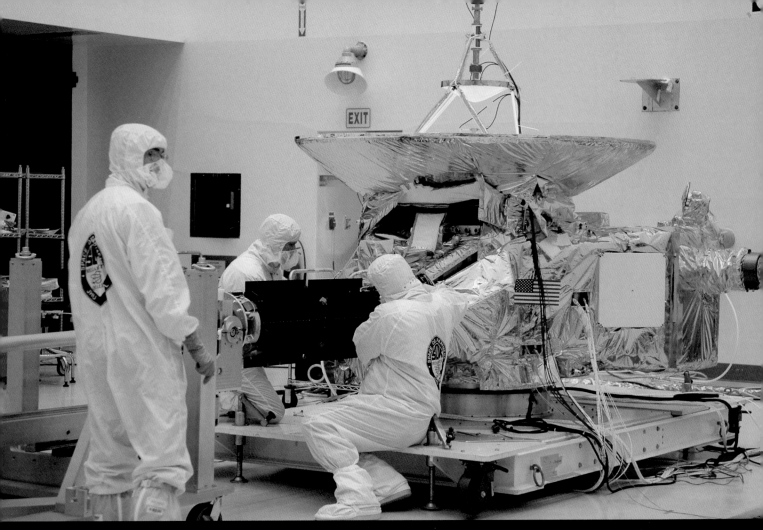

New Horizons was kept in a "clean room" where conditions were almost sterile. No one wanted to send any germs from Earth into outer space. Here engineers, wearing sterile suits, install a specialized generator which provides heat and power to the spacecraft on its long journey to Pluto and beyond. The gold foil is the top layer of many layers of thin protective insulation that keeps the spacecraft at an even temperature and offers it some protection from dust particles in space.

trometer Science Investigation, is a long name for a small instrument that weighs only 3.3 pounds (1.5 kilograms). PEPSSI studies the atoms that escape from Pluto's atmosphere. It was able to detect and count these particles while New Horizons was still far away from Pluto. This information allowed scientists to understand more about what is in Pluto's atmosphere, and how quickly it is escaping into space.

The final instrument is called the Student Dust Counter, or SDC for short. It was designed by students who were studying physics at the University of Colorado, as part of the New Horizons Education and Public Outreach project. The SDC is the first NASA mission instrument designed, built, and managed by students. The SDC measured and counted the dust grains produced by collisions among asteroids, comets, and other objects along New Horizons's path as it made its long journey to the Kuiper Belt.

Of course, any instrument needs electricity to run it. Most space missions use solar power—the energy produced by the sun—to create energy for the spaceship. But New Horizons was going to travel so far away from the sun that solar energy wouldn't work. Furthermore, the instruments on board had to last for *years*, not mere days or even months, as previous missions had needed to. So engineers on the team designed instruments that were extremely energy efficient, and they used a special kind of generator on New Horizons to power those instruments. All together, the seven instruments require about twenty-eight watts to run—that's not much more than it takes to power a lightbulb on Earth.

All this equipment—called the science payload—is tucked inside the spacecraft and managed by an onboard computer that collects and processes the information, sends it back to Earth, and receives commands from scientists at mission control. And there is one other interesting item on board the small craft: human ashes.

The ashes are part of the remains of Clyde Tombaugh, the self-taught astronomer who discovered Pluto. These words are inscribed on the small container that holds them: *"Interred*

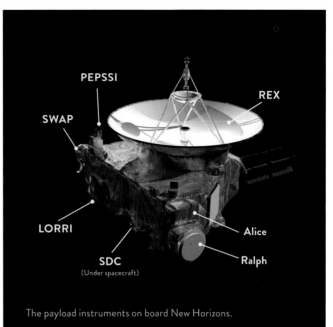

The payload instruments on board New Horizons.

herein are remains of American Clyde W. Tombaugh, discoverer of Pluto and the solar system's 'third zone,' Adelle and Muron's boy, Patricia's husband, Annette and Alden's father, astronomer, teacher, punster, and friend. Clyde W. Tombaugh (1906–1997)." Tombaugh's daughter, Annette, said, "My dad would be thrilled with New Horizons. To actually see the planet that he had discovered and find out more about it, to get to see the moons of Pluto . . . He would have been astounded."

As it turns out, the entire world has been astounded—and fascinated—by this mission to the most distant part of our solar system. Pluto had been a mystery since Tombaugh discovered the tiny space rock on February 18, 1930. However, mysteries need to be solved, and New Horizons was on its way.

2

About Pluto . . .

CLYDE TOMBAUGH WAS not the first person to look for a ninth planet in our solar system. In 1905, Percival Lowell, a wealthy business-man and amateur astronomer, had predicted there was one. For years he had been studying irregularities ("perturbations," as astronomers call a movement outside the norm) in the orbits of Uranus and Neptune. Lowell was convinced these perturbations were caused by the influence of another, unseen planet. He even gave it a name—Planet X. Lowell was so sure of Planet X's existence, he spent years and much of his fortune to build, and then support, the Lowell Observatory in Flagstaff, Arizona.

Years passed, and no one spotted Planet X. And then, in 1929 Clyde Tombaugh arrived at the observatory. He was a young man, just twenty-two years old. He loved to observe the night sky, but his family had no money to send him to college to study astronomy. So, with encouragement from his father and his uncle, Clyde Tombaugh taught himself. He borrowed books from local libraries and read them. He built his own telescope, using parts from his father's farm machinery. He made careful drawings of what he observed with that telescope, and he sent those drawings to the Lowell Observatory. The drawings were so good, the professional

Percival Lowell spent years at his observatory, looking for Planet X.

astronomers who worked there offered young Clyde a job! And so he moved to Flagstaff.

Clyde Tombaugh's job at the Lowell Observatory wasn't peering through a telescope to study the heavens. Instead, he was to sit at a bench and compare identical pictures of the night sky, taken several days apart. His job was to use a piece of equipment called a blink comparator to rapidly flip back and forth between the two photographs. He was looking for a change—something that appeared to move across the night sky. He did this work for the next year, carefully comparing hundreds of pictures with thousands of stars in them. The work bored him. He considered quitting. He asked himself, "Do I want to go through this very tedious job or not?" Fortunately, he decided to continue, saying later, "I liked the work, really, and I was very, very careful."

Tombaugh's patience and care finally paid off. The pictures made on the night of January 23, 1930, then again on January 29, showed a change. Out of the thousands of stars in the seemingly identical images, something was different. An object had moved from one point to another against the background of stars. That "something" was a planet. Clyde Tombaugh had discovered Planet X. Other astronomers checked and rechecked Tombaugh's work. No one said anything for a while. They wanted to

Clyde Tombaugh working with the Zeiss Comparator at the Lowell Observatory. Tombaugh operated the comparator by turning a small dial that flipped a mirror back and forth between the two images.

be absolutely sure of what they were seeing in the photographs. At last, on March 13, 1930—which would have been Percival Lowell's seventy-fifth birthday—they were ready to make the announcement. Earth had a new planet in its solar system, and Clyde Tombaugh had discovered it. Later in his life, as he thought about this moment, Clyde Tombaugh said, "I realized in a few seconds' flash that I'd made a great discovery, that I'd become famous, and I didn't know what would happen after that. It was a very intense thrill."

What happened after that was worldwide excitement. There were now nine known planets orbiting Earth's star, the sun. A name like Planet X didn't seem appropriate, so a contest was held to name the new planet. A young girl in Oxford, England—Venetia Burney—looked

DISCOVERY OF THE PLANET PLUTO

January 23, 1930

January 29, 1930

at her grandfather and simply said, "Why not Pluto?" Pluto was the Roman god of the underworld, a place of the dead that they believed existed somewhere underground. Of course, it was dark and cold in the god Pluto's domain, and astronomers knew it had to be dark and cold around Pluto, since it was so far from the sun's light. The name fit.

Venetia's grandfather knew important astronomers in England and the United States. He sent word of his granddaughter's suggestion to Herbert Turner at the Royal Observatory, who in turn sent the suggestion to the Lowell Ob-

servatory in Arizona. In May 1930, it became official: Planet X was now known as Pluto.

Schoolchildren memorized this silly sentence, or one like it: *My very educated mother just served us nine pizzas.* The first letter of each word stood for the name of a planet, in the order of its distance from the sun. Mercury, the planet closest to the sun, was first, followed by Venus, Earth, Mars, Jupiter, Saturn, Uranus, Neptune, and finally, Pluto. That sentence worked well until August 24, 2006. New Horizons was already on its way when poor Pluto was demoted.

The plates that found Pluto. The arrows point to a tiny dot, but one that has moved across the night sky.

rings and astounding moons.
Since 1993 JPL's Wide-Field and Planetary Camera (WFPC2) on NASA's Hubble Space Telescope has continued to observe Uranus.

In 1989 Voyager 2 sped past Neptune (top right), discovering narrow rings and many small satellites. Neptune is the windiest planet, with winds blowing at speeds over 2,400 kilometers (1,500 miles) per hour.

Distant Pluto and its moon Charon— 30 to 50 times farther from the Sun than Earth is– have not been visited by spacecraft. The European Space Agency's Faint Camera on NASA's Hubble Space Telescope provided this view (bottom).

Planetary Science Professor Michael Brown, who heads the California Institute of Technology (Caltech) Planetary Astronomy Group, in 2005. In 2010 he wrote a book, *How I Killed Pluto and Why It Had It Coming*. His discovery of Eris led to Pluto's eventual demotion.

Mike Brown is the astronomer most people blame for Pluto's demotion from planet to dwarf planet. Mike had been looking for other planets when, like Clyde Tombaugh, he discovered another celestial body. At first Mike thought he had discovered the tenth planet of our solar system, and he submitted his information to the International Astronomical Union (IAU), a body of astronomers from around the world who are in charge of (among other things) naming bodies in space. The IAU named Mike's discovery Eris. But a funny thing happened on the way to Eris becoming a planet.

When Mike Brown submitted his work on Eris, the IAU realized that there was no "official" definition for the word *planet*. So they decided to create one. In order to be a planet, they said, a celestial body had to have three characteristics. It had to: 1) orbit the sun, 2) be round, or almost round, because it had enough gravity to pull it into that shape, and 3) travel in an orbit by itself, like a runner on a racetrack, and clear its neighborhood of other objects.

And then, as the IAU applied its new definition to Eris, the group gave some thought to Pluto. Pluto orbited the sun. Pluto was round. But neither Pluto nor Eris was big enough—had enough gravity—to "clear its neighborhood" of other objects. In other words, to be a planet, an object had to have enough gravity to either pull other objects into itself, make moons out of

Charles Bolden was an astronaut for 14 years before being named Administrator of NASA. He retired from that post in January 2017.

them, or just sling them out of the way. However it happened, the IAU said a planet had to be the biggest, strongest object in its orbit. Pluto and Eris had a problem. They are orbiting in the Kuiper Belt, way beyond Neptune, and the Kuiper Belt is full of millions of icy and rocky objects. Pluto and Eris are just two of them.

The IAU reasoned that Eris, and now Pluto, were not behaving like the other eight planets in Earth's solar system. The organization decided their members needed to come up with a new category for celestial bodies that didn't occupy their own "lane" but still were round, orbited the sun, and were not moons or satellites of another planet. They decided to call any object that fit this definition a dwarf planet. Eris, they said, was a dwarf planet. And so was Pluto.

When New Horizons lifted off its launchpad, Pluto was a full planet. Now, seven months after launch, it was not.

Pluto's demotion shocked the world. Mike Brown said he gets a lot of angry e-mails from schoolchildren who blame him, because it was his discovery of Eris that led to the demotion of Pluto. He laughed about this, and said he thinks the IAU made the right decision. "Pluto is not a planet," he said. "There are finally, officially, eight planets in the solar system."

Alan Stern disagreed. When the announcement was made, he said, "I'm embarrassed for astronomy." Other astronomers have made comparisons between planets and plants. They say a dwarf fruit tree is still a fruit tree. They reason a dwarf planet is still a planet. Charles Bolden, who was the administrator of NASA at the time, said, "I call it a planet, but I'm not the rule maker."

So, is Pluto a dwarf planet or a planet? And does it really matter? Pluto still captures the imagination of people everywhere. Everyone was eager to learn more about this icy world, so very far away from our home planet. The world's press covered the launch, as New Horizons finally headed in Pluto's direction. There were hazards ahead on the long journey, but Pluto was out there, and it was time for exploration.

3
WHERE IN THE WORLD IS PLUTO?

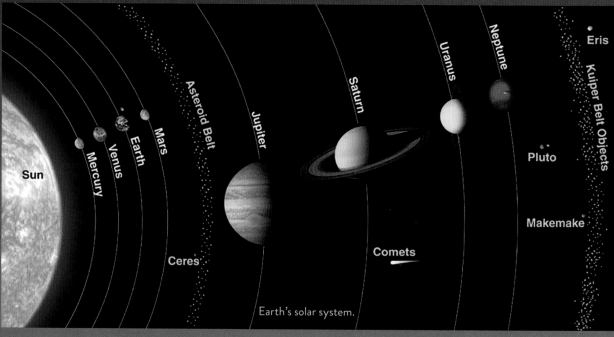

Earth's solar system.

UNTIL 1951, ASTRONOMERS taught that there were four inner "rocky" planets: Mercury, Venus, Earth, and Mars. Those planets made up the first zone of our solar system. The second zone contained the four outer "gas giants": Jupiter, Saturn, Uranus, and Neptune. And there was one small misfit: Pluto. Astronomers knew very little about it, other than that it was so far away, so little, and at the time, it seemed, so alone. Although astronomers had wondered if anything else was out there around Pluto, no one had ever seen a single thing. Pluto didn't fit into the first zone or the second zone, but the tiny icy rock just didn't seem to deserve an entire zone of its own—though one had been suggested.

In 1943, Irish astronomer Kenneth Edgeworth had an idea. Was Pluto really alone, or could there be a vast region of comets and other icy objects located far beyond Neptune? Edgeworth's idea didn't receive much attention until 1951, when a Dutch American astronomer, Gerard Kuiper, also suggested there could be a large doughnut-shaped belt, full of comets, asteroids, and other icy celestial bodies, located at the very outer edge of our solar system, in the area where our sun's energy and gravity begin to have less influence. Of course, in science, it isn't enough to "mention" or "suggest" an idea. Scientists create hypotheses, which are a way of guessing the answer to a question they have. However, proof is necessary for science, and hypotheses need to be proved. Other scientists must test the idea—over and over again. If the results from all these tests are the same, the hypothesis can become a scientific theory—something generally accepted as true. Theories can change, however, if new information becomes available.

In 1992, after almost five years of searching, and forty-one years after Gerard Kuiper proposed his hypothesis, astronomers Dave Jewitt and Jane Luu discovered a tiny reddish speck way beyond Neptune and much farther away than Pluto! It seemed that Gerard Kuiper had been right. Jewitt and Luu nicknamed their discovery Smiley, and it became the first Kuiper Belt Object (KBO). Eventually Smiley got an official designation: 1992 QB1.

More discoveries followed. In 2005, Mike

Gerard Kuiper, taught at the University of Arizona. By all accounts, he was a demanding professor who expected excellence from his students.

Brown, Chad Trujillo, and Dave Rabinowitz announced their discovery of Eris, which is named after the Greek goddess of discord. The name seems appropriate, since we know what happened to Pluto as a result!

In science, it is important to publish information about new discoveries that are made, so other scientists can review and check the work. There are some doubts as to who actually discovered the next Kuiper Belt Object. A Spanish team claims they observed it first in 2003. But they didn't publish anything about their findings that year. Mike Brown's team from CalTech claims they were first, and it wasn't discovered until 2005. Brown's team published their research in 2005. They named the object Haumea (HOW-me-ah), after the Hawaiian goddess of fertility.

In 2012, David Jewitt, Jane Luu, and Mike Brown's work earned the distinguished Kavli Prize in Astrophysics "for discovering and characterizing the Kuiper Belt and its largest members, work that led to a major advance in the understanding of the history of our planetary system."

Mike Brown and his team discovered Makemake (MAH-kee MAH-kee) in March 2005, too. Nicknamed Easterbunny at first, Makemake officially took the name of the fertility god of the Rapanai people from Easter Island in the southeastern Pacific Ocean. Eventually Eris, Haumea, and Makemake would all be declared dwarf planets. With the discovery of three new dwarf planets—four, when you add Pluto—our solar system now had an official third zone. Pluto's neighborhood, the Kuiper Belt, was pretty crowded. And what of the Irish astronomer, Kenneth

Edgeworth, who started the conversation? In his honor, some refer to the Kuiper Belt as the Edgeworth-Kuiper Belt. His contribution has not been forgotten. Although they did not live to know for sure whether their hypotheses would be proved or not, both Edgeworth and Kuiper had been correct.

So, how far away are Pluto and the Kuiper Belt? Distances in the solar system are measured in astronomical units, or AU. An AU is the distance between the Earth and the sun. Earth is almost 93 million miles (150 million kilometers) away from the sun, or 1 AU. Be-

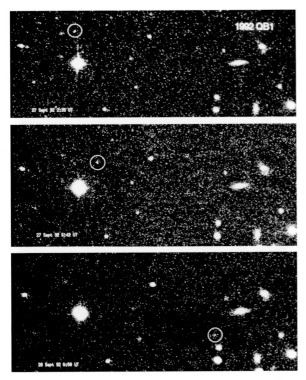

The first Kuiper Belt Object—1992 QB1—was discovered in 1992 by American astronomers David Jewitt and Janet Luu using the 2.2-m telescope at Mauna Kea in Hawaii. Note its movement across the night sky.

cause of its wild orbit, Pluto, on the other hand, comes as close to the sun as 2.7 billion miles (4.3 billion kilometers), or about 29.7 AU, and it travels as far away as 4.7 billion miles (7.6 billion kilometers)—49.3 AU. Earth is close enough to the sun to make a complete orbit in one calendar year, while Pluto needs 248 years to make the same trip around our star. Pluto is so far away, if you tried to ride a bike, it would take you 47,600 years to get there! If you rode in a jet plane, the trip would last 700 years, and even if you were traveling in a spaceship like the old space shuttle, it would take you 25 years to arrive.

With these distances, it's easy to understand why this part of our solar system has never been explored—at least, until now. Alan Stern says, "This is a whole new class of worlds. To understand the solar system, we need to understand worlds like Pluto."

There are many reasons to explore Pluto and the other KBOs. We know a lot about the rocky and gas giant planets in our solar system. But the Kuiper Belt is a new frontier in astronomy. To Alan Stern, "The outer solar system is a wild, woolly place. . . . It's wide-open. You get to be the first to do things."

It's true that Pluto had never been explored, and neither have any of its neighbors in the Kuiper Belt. Astronomers believe this region is full of millions of celestial objects, such as dwarf planets, moons, comets, asteroids, meteoroids, and other space debris, including particles so small they are like space dust. Scientists believe the eight planets of Earth's solar system formed from space debris like what is in the Kuiper Belt. They wonder if they will find planetary embryos—planets in the process of forming—that somehow stopped their formation around 4 billion years ago, while our eight planets went right on

An artist's concept of a trans-Neptunian object, three billion miles away from the sun, which is shown as a bright star

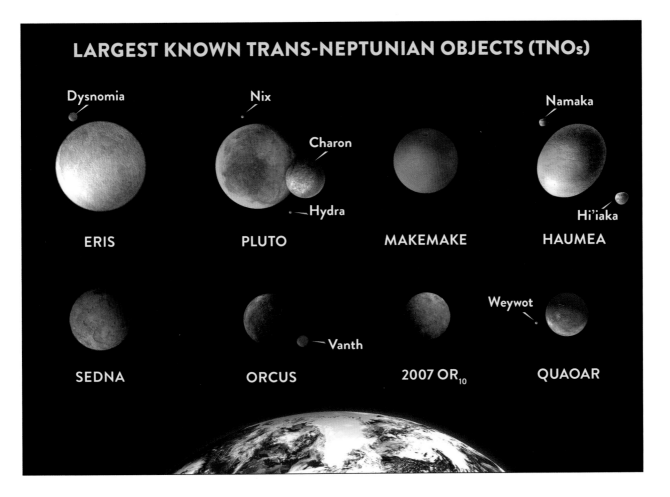

LARGEST KNOWN TRANS-NEPTUNIAN OBJECTS (TNOs)

Dysnomia

ERIS

Nix

Charon

Hydra

PLUTO

MAKEMAKE

Namaka

Hi'iaka

HAUMEA

SEDNA

Vanth

ORCUS

2007 OR$_{10}$

Weywot

QUAOAR

developing. Why would some become planets, while others did not? Studying Pluto and other KBOs will allow us to understand more about how our planet, and the others in our solar system came to exist.

New Horizons also had a chance to study a binary planet for the first time. *Binary* means something has two parts. In this case, Pluto and its largest moon, Charon, are locked together like two ballroom dancers, as they orbit in space. One day on Pluto is equal to six days and nine hours of Earth time. Charon is locked to Pluto in this binary system, so it takes Charon six days and nine hours to orbit around Pluto. As a result, if you were standing on Pluto looking out at Charon, this moon wouldn't appear to move in the night sky. Unlike Earth's moon, Charon is always in the same place in the sky.

Comparison of the eight largest Trans-Neptunian Objects and their moons. Trans-Neptunian objects (TNO) are any objects in the solar system that orbit beyond Neptune. Pluto is a TNO. At the time this image was created, Pluto only had three known moons.

We know there are many binary stars in our galaxy, and there may be other binary planets, too. Astronomers are eager to learn more about the Pluto-Charon binary system. None of these systems has ever been explored, until now.

Scientists are also interested in the asteroids, meteoroids, and comets—"impactors," as they are often called—that form in the Kuiper Belt. These impactors whizzed through the developing solar system, and in its early stages slammed into newly forming objects, like Earth's moon and even Earth itself. New Horizons was equipped to study the craters on Pluto, hoping to learn more about the activity that was taking place there, as our solar system formed.

Even though Kuiper Belt Objects have only been observed from Earth, or with the Hubble Space Telescope, astronomers have been able to make a hypothesis that certain kinds of KBOs, like Eris and a few others, could contain the building blocks for life—carbon molecules and water ice. All life on Earth contains carbon, so scientists study carbon molecules to learn more

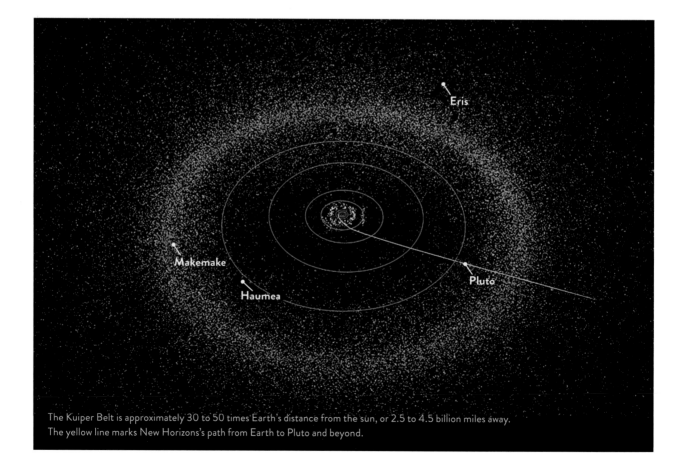

The Kuiper Belt is approximately 30 to 50 times Earth's distance from the sun, or 2.5 to 4.5 billion miles away. The yellow line marks New Horizons's path from Earth to Pluto and beyond.

New Horizons was about 3.7 million miles (6 million kilometers) from the binary system
of Pluto and Charon when it took this picture on July 8, 2015.

about life in all its forms, and how it works. New Horizons was looking for evidence of this kind of organic material on the surface of Pluto. The astronomers were not looking for life on Pluto. Earth is the only planet we know of that contains life of any kind. However, by studying organic material in the Kuiper Belt, scientists hope to understand more about how the chemical ingredients that are necessary for life came to Earth.

And finally, the New Horizons mission will complete the United States' investigation of every planet (or former planet) in our solar system. There is much to learn.

4

To Pluto and Beyond . . .

IN ORDER TO leave Earth's gravity, an object must be traveling over 25,000 miles (40,000 kilometers) per hour. This speed is Earth's escape velocity, and it is thirty-three times faster than the speed of sound! Any speed less than that—even by just a few miles per hour—would be slow enough that an object would be pulled into Earth's orbit. It could not break free and soar into the cosmos.

Speed was no problem for New Horizons. It easily broke Earth's escape velocity and achieved an astonishing speed of 36,373 miles (58,537 kilometers) per hour. That was thanks to the mighty Atlas V rocket, with five rocket boosters attached, that lifted it from the launchpad and hurled it into space. At mission control, there were tears and cheers as the excited team watched the ascent. Their patience, and their persistence, had finally paid off. The historic mission was under way.

New Horizons cruised through the first thirteen months of its journey at this incredible speed. As it streaked through space, engineers on Earth spent their time making certain all the instruments were functioning well. And like a driver taking a car down a highway, they made small corrections to its trajectory—the path it was taking—by using the cameras that were part of the onboard instruments to take images of the surrounding stars.

A map of three thousand stars was stored inside these cameras. Ten times a second, they

snapped a wide-angle picture of space. By comparing the location of the stars in that image to those on the onboard map, computers calculated the spacecraft's position and orientation on its journey. If New Horizons was not where engineers wanted it to be, small thrusters could be fired to change its position. There were sun-sensing instruments on board, too. They backed up the star trackers. In an emergency, the sun sensors could use the Earth and the sun

as points of reference. Using these instruments, engineers on the ground could determine precisely where New Horizons was, anywhere on its journey.

The space probe continued racing toward Jupiter and the sought-after gravity assist.

New Horizons reached its first destination on February 28, 2007, exactly as planned. When it approached, the spacecraft began to feel the pull of Jupiter's gravity, causing it to

Mission Control for New Horizons's one-way journey into outer space.
Here engineers send and receive commands to and from the spaceship.

New Horizons flew over Jupiter's Little Red Spot on its way to Pluto.

speed up as it moved toward the planet, just as you speed up when riding a bike downhill. Of course, you slow down when pedaling uphill, so gravity works both ways! Jupiter was in the right position in its orbit to allow New Horizons to "tag along" for a while, before being "slung away" (like a slingshot) toward Pluto. That maneuver picked up an additional 8,950 miles (14,400 kilometers) per hour for New Horizons. The additional speed cut three to five years off the voyage. It had only eight years and four months to go.

No scientist likes to waste an opportunity to explore something new, so scientists had programmed New Horizons's instruments to learn more about the weather on Jupiter. For the first time ever, they were able to see lightning strikes in Jupiter's polar regions. They were able to measure the size and speed of the "waves" that streak across the width of Jupiter's surface, indicating violent storms below. And New Horizons took the first close-up images of Jupiter's Little Red Spot, which revealed a storm about the size of Earth, as compared to Jupiter's Great Red Spot, another storm, which is about three times the size of our planet. By the time this information reached the eager scientists on Earth, New Horizons had left Jupiter behind. It was put into hibernation—a state where it used as little energy as possible—as it cruised

Jupiter's moon, Io, is slightly larger than Earth's moon and is the most volcanically active body in the entire solar system. New Horizons captured this image of the volcano Tvashtar spewing its plumes 200 miles into space. In this image, the plumes appear blue.

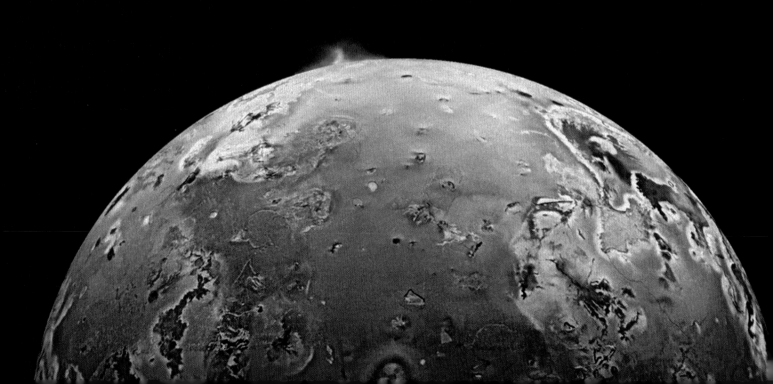

Lava spills over the surface of Io, one of Jupiter's moons.

671 million miles (1,080 million kilometers) per hour, or 186,000 miles (299,000 kilometers) per second. Traveling at that speed, you could circle Earth at its equator seven and a half times in one second! Even at the speed of light, it took four hours and twenty-five minutes to get messages back to Earth from Pluto. The team on the ground was eager to hear from their spacecraft, and fearful they would not, so they waited with anticipation and dread.

Alan Stern was excited as he waited. He compared Pluto and its moons to Christmas presents, just waiting to be unwrapped. He said all the studies of Pluto that had been done up to now were like shaking a wrapped box, wondering what was inside. "I've been waiting twenty-six years to unwrap these presents. This year, Christmas comes in July."

Still, there was danger. There is leftover dust in space. New Horizons was going so fast (nine miles per second!) that if it collided with a bit of space dust no larger than a grain of rice, the results would be horrible. New Horizons could tumble uncontrollably and be knocked off its trajectory so badly, it could never recover and get back on course. As New Horizons got closer and closer to Pluto, the team on Earth used its instruments to scour the area, looking for anything that might be an obstacle, hoping to find a way to avoid it in time. Alan Stern

along toward Pluto. In fact, New Horizons spent almost two-thirds of its time on the long journey taking a nap! During hibernation, most of its instruments and computer systems were shut down—to reduce wear and tear over the long flight. Still, the spacecraft was programmed to send a signal back to Earth once a week, as if to say, "I'm okay." And engineers at mission control "woke it up" every four to six months, to be sure it was still all right.

New Horizons hibernated and woke up eighteen times over the course of its journey to Pluto. Each time, anxious scientists on Earth waited to hear from their spacecraft. Waiting was stressful. It took hours to get a signal back from space, even though that radio signal was traveling at the speed of light, which is about

Interstellar dust often forms into a cloud such as this one; however individual particles of dust are spread throughout the cosmos and can be dangerous to space travel.

had put the odds of losing New Horizons in a collision with a piece of space debris at one in ten thousand, but still, everyone was tense as the craft closed in on Pluto.

Finally, on July 14, 2015, New Horizons flew just 7,800 miles (12,500 kilometers) above Pluto's surface. It was traveling at 30,000 miles (48,000 kilometers) per hour, and it passed Pluto in just three minutes! Of course, New Horizons was taking pictures of Pluto and its moons as it approached the system, and it continued to take photographs and collect information as it pulled away. So why didn't it go into orbit, or even land there?

Simply put, New Horizons just didn't have the brakes to do it.

Pluto is tiny; therefore its gravity is weak. There wasn't enough gravitational force to help pull New Horizons toward the planet's surface. And New Horizons couldn't slow down on its own and slip into an orbit around Pluto, either. It isn't easy to slow down a spaceship. The complicated process requires a lot of fuel to fire thrusters that would then act as brakes, reversing the forward movement. Carrying that extra three tons of fuel would have slowed down the spaceship and made the journey to Pluto impossibly long. So, with no way to brake and no orbiting possible, the New Horizons team had to be satisfied with a flyby. However,

the team was more than just satisfied. They were excited. And proud. And curious. And hopeful. They were making history, too.

New Horizons was the first spacecraft to explore the dwarf planet, and it will probably be the last one to go there for a very long time. This mission completed NASA's New Frontiers program. So what did they find in Pluto's world of dwarf planet and moons?

Immediately before New Horizons "phoned home" from Pluto, members of the science team waited anxiously (top). As soon as the signal reached Earth, cheers erupted everywhere (bottom).

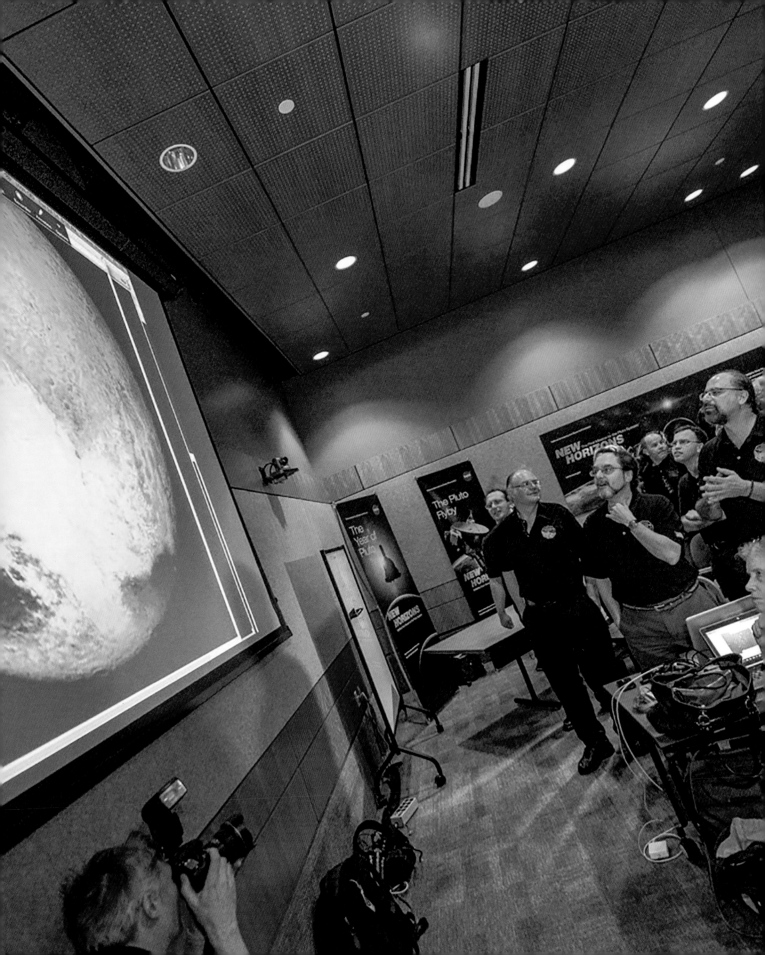

5

A Star of the Solar System

WHEN JIM GREEN, the director of planetary science at NASA, spoke about all the new information that was coming down to Earth, he said, "The New Horizons mission has taken what we thought we knew about Pluto and turned it upside down." Alan Stern added, "It's hard to imagine how rapidly our view of Pluto and its moons is evolving as new data stream in each week. . . . Pluto is becoming a star of the solar system."

Ever since Clyde Tombaugh's discovery of Pluto, scientists have been curious about this tiny piece of rock in outer space. Was it really rock? Or just ice? Was anything happening on it? It had a thin atmosphere, but did that atmosphere produce any weather? And how many moons did Pluto really have? These were just a few of the questions that now had some answers.

The new science tells us that Pluto's surface is changing, just

An eager team of New Horizons engineers watches as the first close-up of Pluto appears on the screen.

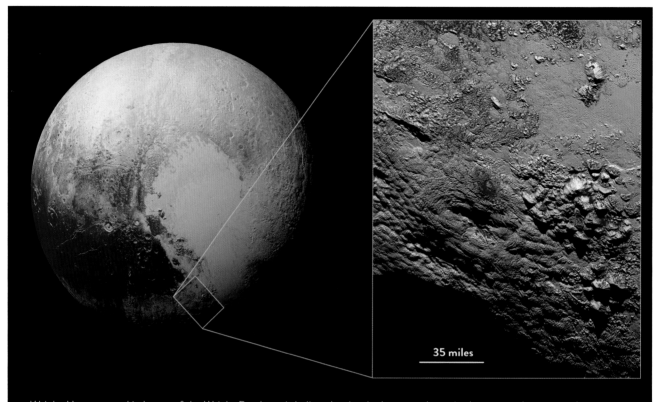

35 miles

Wright Mons, named in honor of the Wright Brothers, is believed to be the largest volcano in the outer solar system. It measures 90 miles across and rises 2.5 miles above Pluto's surface. Because there is only one impact crater, scientists believe the volcano is relatively young.

like Earth's surface has changed over millions of years. On Earth, glaciers moved, volcanoes erupted, earthquakes shook, and waters flooded the surface again and again, over millions of years. Dry land appeared where there had been sea. Mountains thrust up from level ground. Volcanoes spewed lava into the sea, and new land formed. The process, called geological activity, continues today. A geologist would say Earth is a *dynamic* planet, meaning it is constantly changing. So is Pluto. And volcanoes seem to be contributing to the process there, just as they do on Earth.

Earth's volcanoes spew out melted rock, or lava. Pluto's volcanoes seem to be erupting a mushy substance (somewhat like a Slurpee) that consists of water ice, nitrogen, ammonia, or methane. More study is needed. While volcanoes have been studied on other, closer planets, nothing like these kinds of volcanoes has ever been seen this far out in the solar system. Their existence has surprised many researchers.

On Pluto, the gray plains of Sputnik Planitia meet red highlands known as Krun Macula. Krun is the name of the god of the underworld in the Mandaean religion, and a macula is a dark spot.

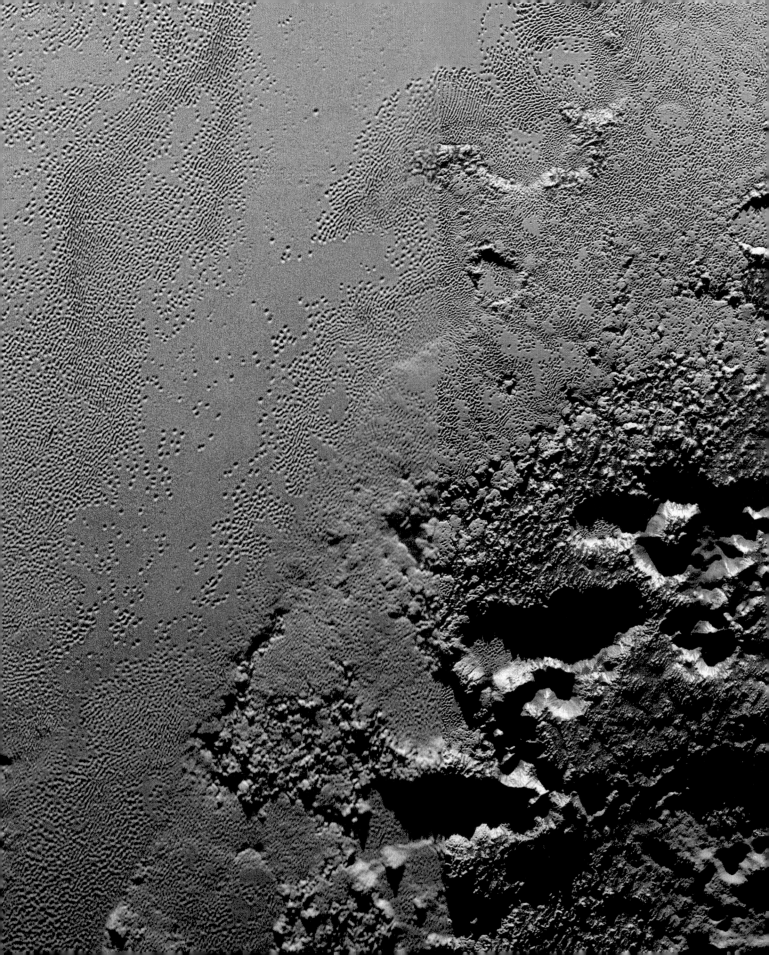

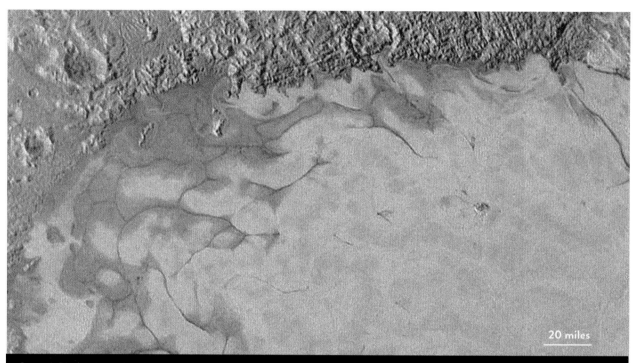

20 miles

Sputnik Planitia is marked by several icy hills, that scientists believe are fragments of the water ice that makes up the surrounding uplands, or mountains. Challenger Colles, named for the astronauts who perished in the *Challenger* explosion, is a large accumulations of these hills. Scientists believe these icy hills are floating on Sputnik Planitia's nitrogen "sea" and are behaving much like icebergs do on Earth.

Pluto's volcanoes are relatively young, also. They probably formed no more than 100 million years ago, which is yesterday in geological time. By comparison, other parts of Pluto are ancient, and probably came together about 4 billion years ago. You may wonder how scientists can tell the age of something that is in outer space. Counting craters is one way to do it, and that is the method the New Horizons team relied upon.

The story of our planets and their moons begins around 4.6 billion years ago. Back then, there was a lot of activity in the future solar system. Meteoroids, comets, and other objects whizzed around. Some of this cosmic debris crashed into the still-forming planets and their moons. The impacts from the flying debris caused craters—depressions on the surface, or crust, of the objects they hit. But the debris storm didn't last forever. Scientists reason that heavily cratered surfaces, such as the far side of Earth's moon, probably existed during the period of bombardment. That makes them old. Newer surfaces, which are smooth, came into being after the bombardment stopped. Parts of Pluto are smooth, and probably formed after

Scientists are interested in the layered craters that dot Pluto's icy plain.

the debris storm was over. Other parts of Pluto are heavily cratered. Those are the ancient surfaces, dating from the time the solar system was forming.

So Pluto's cratered surfaces are old, but its volcanoes and part of its now-famous "heart," Sputnik Planitia (originally named Sputnik Planum) are young. Geologists say the plains of Sputnik Planitia are only 10 million years old—practically new in geological terms.

Sputnik Planitia is a smooth glacier made of soft nitrogen ice that has been compared to the consistency of toothpaste or hot wax. There is not a crater in sight, which indicates that this area formed long after the early chaos and bombardment stopped, making it relatively new in Pluto's development. Right now scientists think Sputnik Planitia may be the largest glacier in the entire solar system!

Pluto's moons provided other surprises. When New Horizons left the launchpad in 2006, Pluto was still a planet, and everyone thought it had three moons: Charon, Nix, and Hydra. But over time, our understanding of how things work, and even what things are, can change. During New Horizons's long voyage, Pluto was demoted to a dwarf planet, but its moon count got promoted from three to five. Kerberos, the fourth moon, was discovered in 2011, and then Styx appeared in 2012. The New Horizons team anticipated discovering even more moons as the spacecraft drew close to Pluto. But science is never certain, which is what makes it exciting. There were no other moons. Using crater counting and the images taken by New Horizons, scientists have decided that all of Pluto's moons are ancient, and are probably debris that was knocked off Pluto when it collided with another large object during that early bombardment, when things were hitting each other like bumper cars gone crazy.

The moons are also interesting in the way they behave. The four smaller moons tumble and dance around Pluto in a strange pattern not seen anywhere else. Like other moons, they rotate on their axes, the way a top spins around a central point. But they do it in a hurry! Hydra is the fastest. It spins once every ten hours,

CHARON AND THE SMALL MOONS OF PLUTO

Styx   Nix   Kerberos   Hydra

10 miles
10 km

Charon

and it takes thirty-eight days to orbit Pluto.

Pluto's largest moon, Charon, is interesting, too. Up until now, astronomers had assumed it had a smooth surface, but they saw that the moon is pockmarked with craters, and there is a huge slash across it, resembling the Grand Canyon in Arizona. New Horizons's cameras revealed a dark red area on its polar cap. There is nothing like it anywhere else in the solar system, and scientists are still trying to decide what it might be. More study is needed, but for now, they think it could be an accumulation of gases that have escaped from Pluto's atmosphere and gathered again on Charon's pole.

Pluto's atmosphere provided other surprises, too. Like Earth's, it is complex and layered, and has vast changes in its atmospheric pressure. There is weather on Pluto! Photographs returned from New Horizons seem to show clouds in the sky, which indicate weather changes. Alan Stern discussed the possible clouds, but noted that Pluto is 99 percent cloudless. "The situation on Pluto is like that in the western United States, where the skies are not cloudy all day," he said, borrowing some words from an old cowboy song. Nevertheless, he stated that clouds on Pluto would indicate that its weather system is much more compli-

Pluto's five moons. Charon was discovered in 1978. The powerful Hubble Space Telescope discovered Nix and Hydra in 2005, then in 2011 it discovered Kerberos, and in 2012 it found Styx. These are Pluto's only moons.

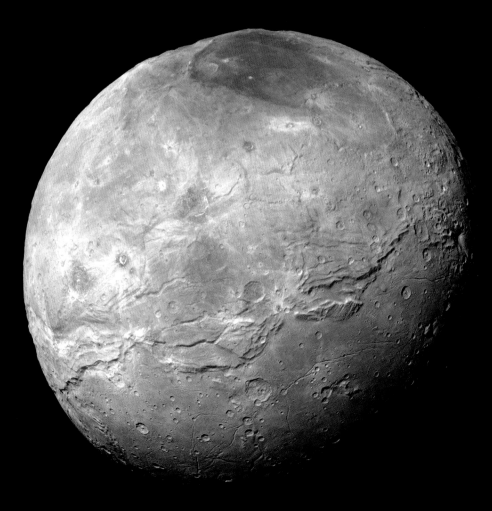

Charon's craters, the deep slash across its center, and the dark red area
of possible tholins show clearly in this image.

Pluto's blue sky, thought to be caused by tholins scattering the sunlight that reaches the tiny dwarf planet.
The definition of "planet" is still under debate. Perhaps Pluto will become a planet once again; perhaps it will not.
Either way, Alan Stern has stated this is his favorite image from the entire flyby.

cated than anyone thought before New Horizons made its flyby.

Finally, and perhaps most surprisingly, Pluto is colorful! The surface is reddish brown, and the color of its sky surprised everyone. "Pluto's sky is blue!" Alan Stern exclaimed. "Who would have expected a blue sky in the Kuiper Belt? It's gorgeous!"

On Earth, when a beam of light from the sun (which contains all the colors in a rainbow) reaches our atmosphere, the blue wavelength, which is shorter than any of the other colors, gets scattered by the gases and particles that are in our atmosphere. As a result, we see a blue sky. But on Pluto, the blue sky seems to be a result of light being scattered by tiny soot-like particles called tholins.

Tholins are formed when the sun's ultraviolet light combines with a gas like methane, ethane, or nitrogen. Tholins do not form on Earth—at least, not now. But they are abundant on the surface of icy bodies in the outer solar system, such as Pluto. Some scientists speculate that the raw materials for life could have been brought to Earth by tholin-rich comets.

Michael Summers is a planetary scientist on the New Horizons team who is interested in astrobiology, studying the beginnings of life in the universe. He is excited about the discovery that Pluto has tholins, water ice, mountains,

Pluto and its largest moon, Charon, spin around a common center of gravity.

and complex layers of haze in its atmosphere. He said, "The connection with astrobiology is immediate. It's right there, in front of your face. You see organic materials, water, and energy. I've been studying Pluto all my life, and never expected to talk about these things being there." The possibility of discovering how life—any kind of life—begins and develops away from Earth is exciting and challenging.

This is just a taste of the science that has been returned to Earth from the instruments on board New Horizons. As Jim Green discussed the New Horizons mission, he said, "It's why we explore—to satisfy our innate curiosity and answer deeper questions about how we got here and what lies beyond the next horizon."

6
BEYOND THE NEXT HORIZON

NEW HORIZONS IS not only the fastest spacecraft ever launched, it is also the only craft to have visited Pluto's world. But fortunately, it didn't stop there. As the Pluto mission was planned, Alan Stern and his team knew it could be years—even decades—before another spacecraft like New Horizons would leave Earth on a journey like this. So as they worked on the Pluto part of the journey, they were already planning for New Horizons's next exploration—even before it had left the launchpad, even before they knew whether they would get permission to go farther into deep space. It was wise to plan ahead, because on July 1, 2016, NASA approved and funded an extension to the New Horizons mission.

Thanks to all the prior planning, the cameras mounted inside LORRI and Ralph had

An artist's concept of what 2014 MU69 may look like.

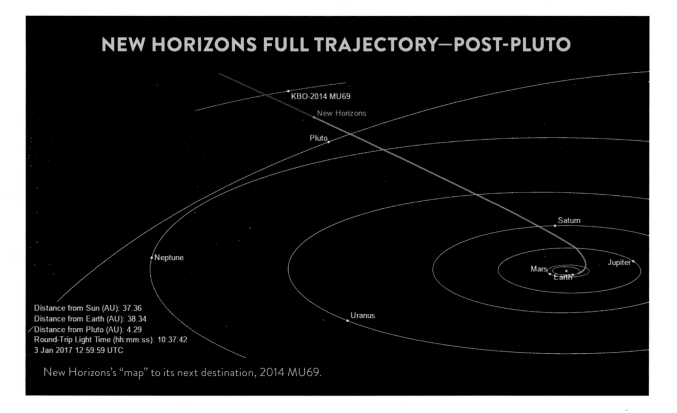

NEW HORIZONS FULL TRAJECTORY—POST-PLUTO

KBO-2014 MU69

New Horizons

Pluto

Saturn

Neptune

Jupiter

Mars
Earth

Distance from Sun (AU): 37.36
Distance from Earth (AU): 38.34
Distance from Pluto (AU): 4.29
Round-Trip Light Time (hh:mm:ss): 10:37:42
3 Jan 2017 12:59:59 UTC

Uranus

New Horizons's "map" to its next destination, 2014 MU69.

already been at work—even before the craft arrived at Pluto—photographing possible places to go, farther out in the Kuiper Belt. Now that they had the funds to continue, the mission team confirmed their target—a small (13 to 25 miles [21 to 40 kilometers] in diameter) icy world lurking another billion miles (1.6 billion kilometers) beyond Pluto, and 4 billion miles (6.4 billion kilometers) from the sun. Its name is 2014 MU69. In September and October 2015 just a few months after receiving permission to go there, New Horizons received commands from mission control to fire a series of four small bursts from the thrusters, which changed its direction. When those firings were

successful, New Horizons headed toward an additional adventure in exploration and discovery. As New Horizons headed deeper into the Kuiper Belt, Jim Green said, "We're excited to continue onward into the dark depths of the outer solar system to a science target that wasn't even discovered when the spacecraft launched."

On January 1, 2019, New Horizons will fly by this distant KBO, which many scientists believe is a leftover from the original formation of our solar system. Perhaps 2014 MU69 will help them understand more about how our solar system—and even life on Earth—came about.

Scientific theories can always change, when

On June 3, 2017 four South African astronomers working in the Karoo Desert of South Africa used portable telescopes to observe 2014 MU69 as it passed in front of a distant star, dimming its light. The event is called occultation. The Milky Way is the white wash in the night sky.

new information is discovered. However, for now, scientists believe our solar system formed about 4.6 billion years ago, as bits of gas, space dust, ice, and rocks, similar to the material in the Kuiper Belt, collected inside a space cloud called a nebula.

That nebula was huge, and because of its size, it had a lot of gravity. Over millions of years, the force of gravity caused the giant cloud to flatten out and start to spin. Picture a lump of pizza dough flattening and expanding into a disk when an expert knows how to spin

it. The flattened-out nebula, which was now a protoplanetary disk, was spinning around our young sun. As the sun grew larger, its gravity pulled some of the material, or matter, in the protoplanetary disk into itself. Earth's star grew bigger and hotter.

However, other bits and pieces of the rock, ice, gas, and dust were farther away from the sun. That distance allowed them to escape the sun's gravity. But the nebula's gravity pulled these bits together into clumps of matter that we now call planets, moons, asteroids, and comets.

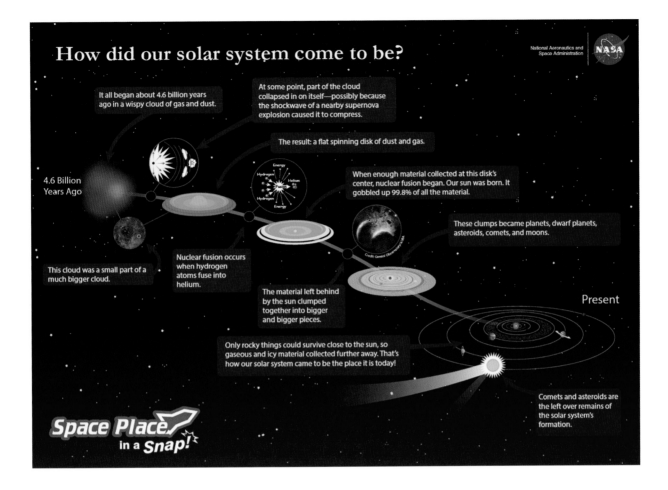

How did our solar system come to be?

National Aeronautics and Space Administration **NASA**

It all began about 4.6 billion years ago in a wispy cloud of gas and dust.

At some point, part of the cloud collapsed in on itself—possibly because the shockwave of a nearby supernova explosion caused it to compress.

The result: a flat spinning disk of dust and gas.

4.6 Billion Years Ago

When enough material collected at this disk's center, nuclear fusion began. Our sun was born. It gobbled up 99.8% of all the material.

These clumps became planets, dwarf planets, asteroids, comets, and moons.

This cloud was a small part of a much bigger cloud.

Nuclear fusion occurs when hydrogen atoms fuse into helium.

The material left behind by the sun clumped together into bigger and bigger pieces.

Present

Only rocky things could survive close to the sun, so gaseous and icy material collected further away. That's how our solar system came to be the place it is today!

Comets and asteroids are the left over remains of the solar system's formation.

Space Place in a Snap!

Finally, when the sun grew large enough to ignite, it fused its hydrogen gas into helium, producing heat and light—sunshine! Charged particles from the sun also created the solar wind, which blasted outward into the new solar system.

Some of the newly formed planets, such as Mercury, Venus, Earth, and Mars, developed closest to the sun. As a result, the sun's heat and wind began to blow away many of the gases these planets had in their atmospheres.

They stopped growing, and became the smaller rocky inner planets of our solar system. But the outer planets were farther away from the sun's energy. It was cooler in that part of space, and the sun's energy and wind took much longer to reach them. Those planets continued to grow, and they retained their gases. They became our outer gas giants—Jupiter, Saturn, Uranus, and Neptune. The Kuiper Belt Objects are even farther away, untouched by all this activity. Scientists believe many of these KBOs are exactly

Our solar system developed from a nebula 4.6 billion years ago.

In 2001, the Hubble Space Telescope took this picture of a protoplanetary disk forming around a new star in the Orion Nebula. This disk is 1,400 light years from Earth. An entire solar system can form from a disk like this.

the way they were right after our solar system began to come together. They are the building blocks of everything we know, and 2014 MU69 may teach us a lot.

Of course, that theory about our solar system's formation raises a question: Earth is in a perfect position—not too close and not too far—from the sun, allowing life to develop on our planet. But could life have formed somewhere else in our solar system, or anywhere else in the cosmos? New Horizons's mission to the Kuiper Belt may help us understand more

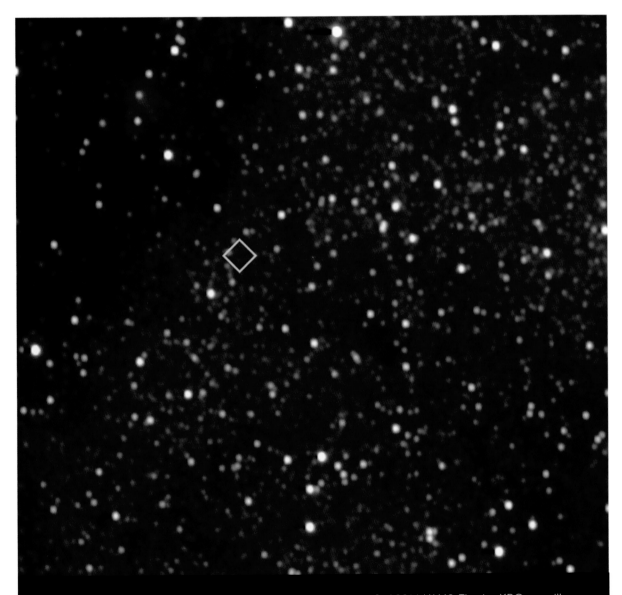

The area inside the yellow diamond is where New Horizons expects to find 2014 MU69. The tiny KBO was still 544 million miles away from New Horizons when LORRI took this picture on January 28, 2017.

about our place here, but the question of life existing anywhere else among the billions of galaxies with their trillions of stars still has no answer. Various theories exist; however, absolutely nothing has been proved. We simply do not know. Nevertheless it is human nature to explore and find out.

On December 17, 1903, Wilbur and Orville Wright became the first people to defy gravity, leave Earth's surface, and fly an airplane into the sky. Almost sixty-six years later, on July 20, 1969, Neil Armstrong took the first step on the moon. Fifty years after that feat, in 2019, instruments aboard a spacecraft created by humans will inspect a piece of space rock that has existed for about 4.6 billion years. It is hard to comprehend our mysterious and magnificent universe, but human beings around the world continue to try. Before the Wright brothers took off, and long before anyone thought about standing on the moon or traveling with New Horizons to the edge of the Kuiper Belt, French scientist Louis Pasteur said, "Science knows no country, because knowledge belongs to humanity, and is the torch which illuminates the world."

Pasteur's words are as true today as they were when he uttered them. The knowledge that humanity gains from New Horizons's voyage will illuminate our understanding of the universe, and light the path to future discoveries.

The Hubble Space Telescope captured this image of 10,000 galaxies which formed a few hundred million years after the Big Bang. The universe is full of mystery.

Pluto, photographed by New Horizons.

FURTHER READING

Bow, James. *New Horizons: A Robot Explores Pluto and the Kuiper Belt*. (Robots Exploring Space). New York: PowerKids Press, 2016.

Buckley, Jr., James. *Curious About Pluto*. New York: Grosset & Dunlap, 2016.

Carson, Mary Kay. *Exploring the Solar System: A History with 22 Activities* (For Kids Series). Revised edition. Chicago: Chicago Review Press, 2008.

Carson, Mary Kay, and Tom Uhlman. *Mission to Pluto: The First Visit to an Ice Dwarf and the Kuiper Belt* (Scientists in the Field Series). New York: HMH Books for Young Readers, 2017.

O'Sullivan, Sandra. *Pluto Welcomes New Horizons: An Historic Adventure in Space*. Dublin: Rockabill Books. April, 2015.

Roland, James. *Pluto: A Space Discovery Guide*. Minneapolis: Lerner Publications, 2017.

Wood, Matthew Brenden. *Planetary Science: Explore New Frontiers* (Inquire & Investigate). White River Junction: Nomad Press, 2017.

WEBSITES OF INTEREST

New Horizons mission:
https://www.nasa.gov/mission_pages/newhorizons/overview/index.html

NASA information for students:
https://www.nasa.gov/audience/forstudents/index.html

Information from the Johns Hopkins Applied Physics Laboratory (JHAPL):
http://pluto.jhuapl.edu/

Learn about astronomy:
https://starchild.gsfc.nasa.gov/docs/StarChild/StarChild.html

Games and interesting information:
https://www.nasa.gov/kidsclub/text/index.html

INDEX

Note: Page numbers in *italics* refer to illustrations.

The plains of Sputnik Planitia are geologically young and active. These blocks of ice, called cells, are turning over in a process called convection in which warmer parts move up, while cooler parts move down, like bubbles in a pot of boiling water on Earth.